The Otherwhere Ice Show

By Gail Kimberly

Illustrated by Mario Capaldi

Dominie Press, Inc.

Publisher: Raymond Yuen
Project Editor: John S. F. Graham
Editor: Bob Rowland
Designer: Greg DiGenti
Illustrator: Mario Capaldi

Published by:

ⵕ Dominie Press, Inc.

1949 Kellogg Avenue
Carlsbad, California 92008 USA

www.dominie.com

1-800-232-4570

Paperback ISBN 0-7685-2074-6
Printed in Singapore
9 10 V0ZF 14 13 12 11 10

Table of Contents

Chapter One
Hard Work Is Good for You......................5

Chapter Two
A Dazzling Smile..9

Chapter Three
As Light as a Snowflake...........................14

Chapter Four
The Ice Show...19

Chapter Five
Grow and Learn...24

Chapter One
Hard Work Is Good for You

The clock struck midnight, but Maggie was still awake, remembering the mistakes she'd made skating at the rink earlier in the day. There were only two weeks left until the Skate Club Ice Show, but she still felt clumsy when she tried to do a double axel.

She could jump from one skate into a turn, but she couldn't complete two turns without falling. With homework and all the other things she had to do, she hadn't practiced enough.

She wanted to practice more. She wanted to go to the frozen pond near her house. She wasn't supposed to go there at night, but her parents were asleep, and she was sure they would understand if they knew how worried she was.

She pulled on her warm pants and a sweater, and then found her gloves and jacket in the bedroom closet. She put on her snow boots and went outside, carrying her skate bag. A full moon glittered on the snowy fields, giving the night a silver brilliance so that Maggie could see her way through the trees and down the lane.

Their house was just outside the city, and in winter Dad smoothed the ice on the pond in the woods so she could skate there. Now it shimmered like a crystal mirror, beautiful but strange at night.

Maggie sat on the wooden bench at the edge of the pond and put on her skates. Dad had made the bench, but Maggie helped, sawing some of the boards and hammering nails. She remembered what Dad said when she complained that it was hard work.

"Hard work is good for you," he said. "It helps you grow and learn."

Maggie laced her skates and took off her jacket, leaving it on the bench. Then she glided out to the center of the pond. She had to practice that double axel until she got it right.

Chapter Two
A Dazzling Smile

Maggie warmed up with figure eights, and then sped across the ice to go into her jump. It was too weak. She stumbled halfway through it and made a clumsy recovery. She circled the pond to try again.

Suddenly a strange voice broke the

silence. Someone was calling to her.

"You're late, Maggie! The show will be starting soon."

Startled, Maggie stared at a tall man who appeared between the trees across the pond. Who was he? What was he doing here?

The man wore a black uniform with sparkling buttons and high, shiny boots. He carried a short whip, like a circus ringmaster. Three tiny women wearing spangled pink gowns appeared beside him and skated toward Maggie. They were shorter than Maggie, although they looked like adults.

Suddenly, there was music coming from nowhere. Icicles on tree branches became spotlights that focused on the center of the pond. The man stepped gracefully across the ice and stood before her. "You need a costume," he said. "You can't perform in those grubby sweats."

"What are you talking about?" Maggie asked, bewildered. "Who are you?"

The man gave her a dazzling smile. He had black curly hair and shining green eyes. He was very tall. Maggie only came up to the second button on his waist-length jacket.

"He's Magnus, of course," one of the little women said.

"Everybody in *Otherwhere* knows Magnus," another said.

"Yes, it's true," the man said. "I'm Magnus, the magician. And you're Maggie Williams."

"How did you know?"

"We know what goes on in your world," he said. "I know you need my help, or I wouldn't be here." He lifted his whip,

and a jewel flashed at the end of it.

"You're Cinderella in the ice show, aren't you?" He waved the whip, and Maggie saw that her clothes had become Cinderella's ragged dress, smeared with soot.

Chapter Three
As Light as a Snowflake

"Now," Magnus said, "for the wicked stepmother and the ugly sisters."

He waved his whip, and the three little women were suddenly dressed in stepsister and stepmother costumes, with makeup hardening their faces into scowls.

The music changed to the Cinderella theme they would play in Maggie's show.

"Are you ready?" Magnus asked her. Maggie felt dazed.

"No," she told Magnus. "Wait. I don't understand what's going on."

"You're not ready? But you've been rehearsing to do Cinderella, haven't you?"

"Yes," Maggie said. She looked down at her new costume, then at the skates on her feet. "But I'm having trouble with the double axel. I haven't had time to practice and get it perfect."

She didn't want Magnus to see her stumble and fall.

"You don't have to practice." Magnus waved his flashing whip above her head.

"There! Now try your double axel." Maggie hesitated.

"Go ahead," he told her, giving her a

nudge toward the center of the ice.

Maggie glided around the pond and built up speed. Her heart jumped into her throat. She could feel it beating harder as she got ready for the jump. Then, almost without trying, she leaped into two perfect turns and landed gracefully. She hardly even felt the landing.

She couldn't believe it had been so easy. Could she do it again?

She raced across the ice and into another perfect double axel, feeling as light as a snowflake and as elegant as a swan. The wicked stepmother and the two ugly sisters applauded her and cheered.

Magnus slapped his whip against his palm. "Are you ready to do the show now? The audience is waiting."

Maggie was confused. What audience was Magnus talking about? He waved his magic whip into the air around the pond. People began to appear and gather around the pond, murmuring and chatting as they settled into rows of benches. Some of them had programs and video cameras.

The pond took on a strange glow, and Maggie found herself in a spotlight. She couldn't tell where the light was coming from. It might have been the Moon.

Maggie blinked at the people. Wasn't that a deer in the front row, with three owls perched on the seats behind it? It was hard to tell with the light shining in her eyes.

Chapter Four
The Ice Show

Magnus stood in the center of the frozen pond. "Ladies and gentlemen, creatures of all ages," he announced, "welcome to the Otherwhere Ice Show!"

He waved his whip. An invisible band played a march and ten small horses with tiny riders appeared from the trees to circle the pond. The horses danced on their hind legs while the riders clasped each other's hands. But were these men riding horses, or were they centaurs, part-horse, part-man? Maggie knew that centaurs were mythical creatures. Nothing was making sense.

The centaurs galloped away, and little clowns in greasepaint and tattered clothes and clumsy shoes ran onto the ice. They tumbled and fought and fumbled and fell while the crowd laughed. After they had performed, small acrobats started swinging from the tree branches on tiny trapezes.

Maggie found herself caught up in the show. She was amazed and frightened by all of the performers. But as she watched, she noticed something about them.

All their faces were unhappy. Even the clowns with happy faces painted on their real faces looked sad somehow. And it made Maggie sad, watching them.

Then Magnus came toward her, his green eyes glowing. "Your turn, Cinderella!"

The crowd was cheering. Yelps and growls, whistles and howls mingled with the music of the Cinderella theme. Magnus took Maggie's hand and led her to the center of the ice.

"Don't be nervous," he whispered. "Remember, my magic will help you do it. With my magic you can do anything."

Maggie glided toward the set where the other skaters were. There was a small fireplace and some chairs. The little wicked stepmother and the ugly sisters waited.

At her cue, Maggie grabbed a broom and skated around them, sweeping.

The other three skaters knew the show as well as she did, and they skated their parts beautifully.

The sets miraculously appeared and disappeared. Their costumes changed into ball gowns as the stepmother and sisters left for the palace. A tiny fairy godmother appeared, and then turned Cinderella into a princess and produced a coach and four dog-sized horses.

Maggie skated better than she ever had, leaping into graceful spins as the spectators applauded wildly. She didn't have to think about her routine. Her feet seemed to know where to go on their own. She felt giddy with excitement.

When she got to the palace, she found that Magnus himself was the prince, and when he danced with her, she glowed with happiness.

Chapter Five
Grow and Learn

Maggie was happy. She had skated a clean routine, and the show was a success.

But deep inside she knew that in spite of the laughter and applause, in spite of the magical beauty of this circus, there was something wrong. The other performers seemed wistful and unhappy. They didn't enjoy the performance as much as she did.

The show came to an end. The audience left as the music faded away, and now the pond was quiet again, shrouded in silent snow.

Maggie stood with the three tiny women and Magnus. "You were wonderful," he told her.

The woman who played the wicked stepmother looked up at her with admiration.

"You were a lovely Cinderella," she said. "I played that part once, long ago, when I was as big as you."

Magnus frowned and brushed her aside. "Will you stay with us?" he asked Maggie. He came closer. "You could star in our show every night."

He was standing right in front of her,
looking down at her. To Maggie's shock,
she saw that she only came up to the
third silver button on his jacket. But she
remembered being as tall as his second
button! She felt a cold chill run down
her spine.

She skated away from Magnus to her
dad's wooden bench, where she sat to

pull off her skates. Magnus followed her.

"Otherwhere is a wonderful place, Maggie," he said. "Everyone gets to do exactly what they want to do. And there is no hard work, no practice. Everyone is a success. There is nothing to worry about. My magic will take care of everything."

Maggie clutched the edge of the bench, remembering what Dad had told her: *Hard work makes you grow and learn.* The people in Magnus's world didn't do any hard work. But they didn't grow and learn, either. In fact, they seemed to be shrinking.

"You need me, Maggie," Magnus told her with a smile. "Without me, you can't do a double axel. Without me, you would trip on your spins. Without me, you would fall right on your face, remember?"

Maggie looked at him. It was true. She had never landed a double axel before his magic helped her. She knew she was getting better, but would she be able to do it by herself?

She skated to the far edge of the pond while Magnus silently watched. She started to pick up speed. Then she prepared to jump.

She lifted off the ground, but it didn't feel right. She spun once, and then fell out of control on the next half-turn and landed with a *smack* on the ice.

Magnus smiled. "You see? You need my magic."

Maggie sat there on the ice where she had fallen. She wanted to cry, but then she remembered why she had come out to the pond in the first place. *Hard work makes you grow and learn.*

She got back up and skated over to Magnus. "I may not be able to do it now," she said. "But I can work on it myself. It might be hard, but I'll get it."

As she spoke, she noticed that Magnus appeared shorter—she was as tall as his second button again.

Magnus shook his head. "You'll never get anywhere without me!" Then he vanished in a puff of smoke.

Maggie looked around. The other skaters were gone and so were the icicle lights. The air was silent, and she had her grubby sweats on again. She skated once around the pond, but she didn't try another double axel that night. The cold air felt good in her lungs.

She glided back over to her dad's bench and sat down. She carefully unlaced her skating boots, took them off,

and put her snow boots on. She looked up and realized just how beautiful the night was in winter.

Then she put her jacket on, put her skates in her bag, and walked back down the path toward home, smiling.